WHAT ARE THE BOOKS OF COLOSSIANS & PHILEMON?

Kids' Guides to God's Word Series

What Is the Book of Genesis?
What Is the Book of Exodus?
What Is the Book of Leviticus?
What Is the Book of Numbers?
What Is the Book of Deuteronomy?
What Is the Book of Joshua?
What Is the Book of Judges?
What Is the Book of Ruth?
What Is the Book of 1 Samuel?
What Is the Book of 2 Samuel?
What Is the Book of 1 Kings?
What Is the Book of 2 Kings?
What Are the Books of 1–2 Chronicles?
What Are the Books of Ezra & Nehemiah?
What Is the Book of Esther?
What Is the Book of Job?
What Is the Book of Psalms?
What Is the Book of Proverbs?
What Is the Book of Ecclesiastes?
What Are the Books of Song of Songs & Lamentations?
What Is the Book of Isaiah?
What Is the Book of Jeremiah?
What Is the Book of Ezekiel?
What Is the Book of Daniel?
What Are the Books of Hosea–Micah?
What Are the Books of Nahum–Malachi?
What Is the Gospel of Matthew?
What Is the Gospel of Mark?
What Is the Gospel of Luke?
What Is the Gospel of John?
What Is the Book of Acts?
What Is the Book of Romans?
What Is the Book of 1 Corinthians?
What Is the Book of 2 Corinthians?
What Is the Book of Galatians?
What Is the Book of Ephesians?
What Is the Book of Philippians?
What Are the Books of Colossians & Philemon?
What Are the Books of 1–2 Thessalonians?
What Are the Books of 1–2 Timothy & Titus?
What Is the Book of Hebrews?
What Is the Book of James?
What Are the Books of 1–2 Peter & Jude?
What Are the Books of 1-3 John?
What Is the Book of Revelation?

What Are the Books of

COLOSSIANS & PHILEMON?

Michael Whitworth

ISBN 978-1-971767-31-4

Published by Start2Finish
Bend, Oregon 97702
start2finish.org

Printed in the United States of America

30 29 28 27 26 1 2 3 4 5

CONTENTS

INTRODUCTION

Have you ever gotten a package in the mail that contained two things that seemed totally different? Maybe it was a birthday gift from a relative: one box held something big and impressive, and tucked beside it was something small and personal, like a handwritten note or a gift card slipped inside an envelope. At first glance, the two items don't seem to go together. One is grand; the other is simple. One is meant for display; the other is meant for your eyes only.

But then you realize they came from the same person, at the same time, for the same reason. And together they say something that neither one could say alone.

That's what you're holding when you read the books of Colossians and Philemon. They're two letters that were written by the same man, sent to the same town, carried by the same messenger, on the same day. One is a sweeping theological masterpiece about the supremacy of Jesus Christ over everything in the universe. The other is a short, personal note asking a friend to forgive a runaway slave. One looks up at the cosmic throne of Christ. The other looks across a kitchen table at a broken relationship that needs to be healed.

And together they answer a question that every Christian has to face: What difference does the gospel actually make?

A LETTER FROM A PRISON CELL

The man who wrote both letters was the apostle Paul, and he wrote them from a prison cell. We don't know for certain which prison. It may have been Rome, where Paul spent two years under house arrest. It may have been Ephesus, a major city in Asia Minor where Paul spent several years and likely faced imprisonment at some point. What we do know is that Paul was in chains. He couldn't travel. He couldn't visit the churches he loved. The most effective missionary the world had ever seen was confined to a small room, watched by guards, unable to go anywhere.

So he wrote letters.

The longer letter went to the church in Colossae, a small city in what is now western Turkey. Paul had never visited Colossae. The church there had been founded by a man named Epaphras, one of Paul's converts, who had carried the gospel back to his hometown and planted a community of believers. Epaphras had recently traveled to Paul with a report: the church was doing well, full of faith and love. But there was a problem. False teachers had shown up, pushing ideas that threatened to pull the Colossians away from the simple truth of the gospel.

We don't know exactly what these teachers were saying. Paul never names them or quotes them directly. But from the way he responds, we can piece together the general shape of their message. They seem to have been telling the Colossians that faith in Jesus was a good start, but it wasn't enough. You also needed to follow certain dietary rules, observe certain religious festivals, practice intense self-denial, and perhaps even worship angels or engage in mystical experiences. Jesus was fine, they implied, but Jesus alone wasn't sufficient.

Paul's response was volcanic. The entire letter to the Colossians is built on one massive idea: Jesus is enough. He is supreme over all creation. All the fullness of God lives in him. You are complete in him. You don't need anything else, anyone else, any other system or practice or philosophy to supplement what Christ has already given you.

That's the big letter. The cosmic one. The one that lifts your eyes to the throne room of heaven and shows you a Christ so enormous that every other claim to power and authority shrinks to nothing beside him.

THE LETTER NOBODY EXPECTED

But tucked alongside that sweeping letter was a second one, small enough to fit on a single sheet of papyrus. It was addressed to Philemon, a Christian leader in Colossae who hosted a church in his home.

The subject? A slave named Onesimus.

Onesimus had belonged to Philemon. At some point, he had run away, possibly stealing money on his way out. He had ended up meeting Paul in prison, and through Paul's ministry, he had become a Christian. Now Paul was sending him back to Philemon with this letter, asking Philemon to do something that would have been almost unthinkable in the ancient world: welcome the runaway slave as a brother.

Not just tolerate him. Not just refrain from punishing him. Welcome him. Embrace him. Treat him as a fellow member of the family of God. And if Onesimus owed Philemon anything, Paul said, put it on my account. I'll pay it.

In twenty-five verses, Paul takes the grand theology of Colossians and brings it down to a single relationship between two real people. If Christ really is supreme over everything, then he's supreme over the master-slave divide too. If God really has reconciled all things through the cross, then reconciliation has to happen in Philemon's living room, not just in the pages of a theology book. If the old divisions of race, class, and status really have been abolished in Christ, then Philemon has to look at Onesimus and see a brother, not a piece of property.

The two letters need each other. Colossians without Philemon might feel abstract—all theory and no practice. Philemon without Colossians might feel like a nice personal request with no foundation underneath it. Together, they show you the full picture: the gospel is both the biggest idea in the universe and the most practical force in your daily life.

WHAT YOU'RE ABOUT TO READ

Here's a roadmap of where we're headed.

Chapters 1–3 walk through the first half of Colossians. You'll watch Paul give thanks for a church he's never visited, pray for their growth, and then unleash one of the most stunning descriptions of Jesus ever written: he is the image of the invisible God, the firstborn over all creation, the one in whom all things hold together. You'll see Paul describe his own suffering and ministry, and you'll discover what he calls "the mystery" of God: Christ in you, the hope of glory.

Chapter 4 takes on the false teaching directly. Paul warns the Colossians not to be taken captive by hollow philosophies and human traditions. He shows them that they are already complete in Christ, that the cross has defeated every rival power, and that the old rules and regulations were only shadows of the reality that has now arrived in Jesus.

Chapters 5–6 cover the second half of Colossians, where Paul describes what the new life in Christ actually looks like. You'll see the famous "take off and put on" passage, where Paul tells Christians to strip away the old patterns of anger, lust, and dishonesty and clothe themselves with compassion, kindness, humility, and love. You'll read his instructions for families, workers, and the church's witness to outsiders. And you'll meet the real people who surrounded Paul: Tychicus, Epaphras, Luke, Mark, and others.

Chapter 7 turns to Philemon, where everything Paul has taught about Christ's supremacy, the new identity of Christians, and the power of forgiveness gets tested in the most personal way possible. Paul asks a friend to do something impossibly hard: to forgive someone who wronged him and to welcome that person as family.

BEFORE WE BEGIN

Before we begin, there's one thing worth knowing. These letters were written nearly two thousand years ago to people living in a culture very different from ours. They lived in a world of slaves and masters, of emperor worship and pagan temples, of small house churches meeting in secret while the Roman Empire stretched across the known world. Some of what Paul says will feel immediately relevant. Some of it will require a little explanation to make sense in your world.

But the core questions these letters address haven't changed. Is Jesus really enough? How do you live when the people around you are pulling you in every direction? What does it look like to forgive someone who has genuinely wronged you? How does what you believe on Sunday morning show up in how you treat people on Thursday afternoon?

Paul answered those questions from a prison cell, with chains on his wrists and fire in his heart. He had given up everything for the gospel, and he wouldn't trade a single day of it. The Christ he describes in these letters isn't a distant idea or a religious concept. He's the living Lord who holds the universe together and who lives inside every person who trusts him.

Two letters. One Christ. And a gospel that changes everything it touches. Let's begin.

Turn the page.

1

A LETTER FROM PRISON

Have you ever gotten a letter or a message from someone you've never actually met? Maybe a pen pal from another country. Maybe a relative who lives far away and sends a card every birthday with your name misspelled. There's something strange about that kind of communication. The person doesn't really know you, but somehow they seem to care about you. They've heard about you from someone else, and what they heard was enough to make them want to reach out.

Now imagine that letter is coming from someone sitting in a prison cell. Not because they did something wrong, but because they did something right. They told the truth, and the truth got them arrested.

That's the situation behind the book of Colossians. The apostle Paul wrote this letter while chained up in a Roman prison. He couldn't travel. He couldn't visit the churches he loved. All he could do was write.

So he wrote. And what he wrote turned out to be one of the most powerful letters in the entire Bible.

Here's what makes Colossians unusual: Paul had never actually been to Colossae. He knew about them because a man named Epaphras, one of his ministry partners, had started the church there. Epaphras came back to Paul with a report: "The church is doing well. They believe in Jesus. They love each other. But there's a problem. Some people are trying to convince them that Jesus isn't enough."

That last part is what made Paul pick up his pen. The idea that Jesus might not be enough was the one thing Paul couldn't let slide. So he wrote a letter to people he'd never met, from a prison cell he couldn't leave, about a Christ who is bigger and more glorious than they had ever imagined.

In this first chapter, before Paul tackles the false teaching, he starts where every good teacher starts: with gratitude and prayer. He thanks God for what he's heard about them. He prays for what he hopes they'll become. And in doing so, he paints a picture of what it looks like when the gospel takes root in someone's life and starts to grow.

HOW ANCIENT LETTERS WORKED

Before we get into the body of the letter, we need to understand how ancient letters worked. In Paul's world, letters started with the sender's name, then the recipients, then a greeting. Paul follows this formula, but he always adds his own twist.

He introduces himself as "an apostle of Christ Jesus by the will of God." An apostle wasn't just a preacher. An apostle was someone personally chosen and sent by Jesus, with authority to speak on his behalf. Paul is reminding his readers right from the start: this letter carries weight. And that authority didn't come from Paul's ambition. It came "by the will of God." Paul didn't choose this job. God chose him for it.

He also mentions Timothy, calling him "our brother." Timothy was one of Paul's closest ministry partners. By including him in the greeting, Paul is saying, "I'm not alone in this. My trusted partner stands with me."

Then Paul describes his audience. He calls them "God's holy people in Colossae, the faithful brothers and sisters in Christ." That word "holy" doesn't mean they were perfect. In the Bible, "holy" means "set apart." It means God has claimed you as his own. The Colossians were holy not because they had earned it, but because God had chosen them. And they were "faithful," meaning they had remained committed to the truth, even when other voices tried to pull them away.

Paul's greeting is short but packed with meaning: "Grace and peace to you from God our Father." Grace is God giving you what you don't deserve. Peace is the wholeness that comes when your relationship with God is right. Those two words sum up pretty much everything Paul believed about the Christian life.

FAITH, LOVE, AND HOPE

After the greeting, Paul does something he does in almost every letter. He prays. And he tells the Colossians exactly what he thanks God for.

"We always thank God, the Father of our Lord Jesus Christ, when we pray for you, because we have heard of your faith in Christ Jesus and of the love you have for all God's people."

Notice how Paul describes God: "the Father of our Lord Jesus Christ." You can't understand who God is apart from Jesus, and you can't understand who Jesus is apart from God. They are bound together.

What has Paul heard about the Colossians? Two things jumped out. First, their faith in Christ Jesus. They trusted him. They believed Jesus was who he said he was and built their lives on that truth. Second, their love for all God's people. Not love for the people they got along with easily. Love for *all* the saints. That kind of love doesn't come naturally. It comes from the gospel doing its work inside you.

But Paul adds a third ingredient: hope. "The faith and love that spring from the hope stored up for you in heaven."

When we hear "hope," we usually think of wishful thinking. "I hope it doesn't rain." But biblical hope isn't crossing your fingers. It's confident expectation based on God's promises. When Paul talks about "the hope stored up for you in heaven," he's talking about something that already exists. It's real. It's waiting. God has set it aside for his people, and nothing can take it away.

Think of it like a Christmas present your parents bought in October and hid in the back of the closet. You haven't opened it yet. You haven't even seen it. But it's there, wrapped and waiting, with your name on it.

And here's what might surprise you: Paul says this hope is the foundation underneath their faith and their love. When you know that your future is secure, it changes how you live right now. You can take risks. You can love sacrificially. You can trust God even when circumstances look terrible, because you know this world isn't all there is.

The Colossians first heard about this hope when Epaphras told them "the true message of the gospel." Paul uses that phrase deliberately. The *true* message. Because other messages were floating around Colossae that twisted the truth. We'll get into those later. For now, Paul wants them to remember where they started: with the genuine, authentic gospel.

A GOSPEL THAT KEEPS GROWING

What Paul says next is easy to read quickly and miss entirely. So slow down. "In the same way, the gospel is bearing fruit and growing throughout the whole world, just as it has been doing among you since the day you heard it and truly understood God's grace."

Paul uses the language of a garden, of seeds and soil and harvest. Those words echo back to Genesis, where God told the first humans to "be fruitful and increase." God's original plan for creation was growth and flourishing. Sin derailed that plan. But the gospel is God's way of getting creation back on track. Through the good news about Jesus, God is filling the world with people who reflect his image.

And it was working. The gospel was crossing borders. It was reaching people nobody expected it to reach. Gentiles in Asia Minor. Slaves in Roman households. Philosophers in Greek cities. And the same power transforming communities across the Roman Empire was at work in their little city too. Their small church in an overlooked town wasn't an afterthought. It was connected to God's plan for the entire world.

Paul says the gospel took root "since the day you heard it and truly understood God's grace." When Epaphras first told them about Jesus, something clicked. They didn't just hear information. They grasped it. And that word "grace" matters.

Grace means the gospel isn't a set of instructions for earning God's approval. It's the announcement that God has already done for you what you could never do for yourself.

"You learned it from Epaphras, our dear fellow servant, who is a faithful minister of Christ on our behalf." Epaphras doesn't get a lot of attention in the Bible. He only shows up in Colossians and in a brief mention in Philemon. But Paul's words here are some of the highest praise he ever gives anyone. "Dear fellow servant." "Faithful minister of Christ."

Epaphras wasn't famous. He wasn't an apostle. He was a regular person who heard the gospel, believed it, and carried it home to his own people. He planted the church, loved them well, and then traveled to Paul to report on how they were doing. He told Paul about their "love in the Spirit," that supernatural affection that only the Holy Spirit can create.

God doesn't need famous people to accomplish his purposes. He needs faithful ones.

WHAT PAUL PRAYED FOR

Now Paul shifts from thanksgiving to prayer. He's told them what he's grateful for. Now he tells them what he's asking God to give them. "For this reason, since the day we heard about you, we have not stopped praying for you. We continually ask God to fill you with the knowledge of his will through all the wisdom and understanding that the Spirit gives."

There it is again: "since the day we heard about you." Paul's response to hearing about the Colossians' faith was to start praying and never stop. A man in a Roman prison, chained and unable to move, praying daily for people he had never met. He didn't see prayer as a nice habit. He saw it as one of the most powerful things he could do.

So what did he pray for?

He asked God to "fill" them with the knowledge of his will. Not a surface-level understanding. He wanted them overflowing with a deep, clear grasp of what God wants and who God is. This knowledge comes "through all the wisdom and understanding that the Spirit gives." Wisdom is the ability to see life from God's perspective. Understanding is the ability to think clearly about how God's truth applies to real situations. Both come from the Holy Spirit. You can't get this kind of knowledge from a textbook or a YouTube video. It's a gift from God.

But knowledge is never the finish line for Paul. It's always the starting point. "So that you may live a life worthy of the Lord and please him in every way." The whole point of knowing God better is to live differently. Paul's prayer is that the Colossians would walk in a way that honors Jesus. Not perfectly. Not flawlessly. But in a way that is "worthy" of him, in a way that reflects his character.

What does that look like? Paul gives four descriptions.

First, "bearing fruit in every good work." A healthy tree produces fruit. A healthy Christian produces good works. Not to earn God's love, but because God's love is already at work inside them. When you truly understand the gospel, good works flow out of you naturally, the way apples grow on an apple tree. The tree doesn't strain to produce fruit. It just does, because that's what healthy trees do.

Second, "growing in the knowledge of God." Knowing God isn't a one-time event. It's a lifelong process. You never stop learning. You never reach the point where you can say, "Okay, I know enough about God." The more you know him, the more you realize there is to know. And the more you know him, the more your life changes. Knowledge fuels obedience. Obedience deepens knowledge. It's a spiral that keeps climbing upward.

Third, "being strengthened with all power according to his glorious might." Living the Christian life isn't easy. Paul knew that better than anyone. He was in prison, after all. Following Jesus will sometimes mean enduring hard things, facing opposition, staying faithful when it would be easier to quit. You need strength for that. But Paul doesn't tell the Colossians to just grit their teeth and try harder. He prays that God would strengthen them with his own power. The same power that created the universe, the same power that raised Jesus from the dead, is available to ordinary people who trust God.

And what is that power for? Not to do flashy miracles. Not to impress people. It's for "great endurance and patience." Endurance is the ability to keep going when circumstances are crushing you. Patience is the ability to keep going when people are driving you crazy. Both require supernatural strength. Both are marks of genuine faith.

Fourth, "giving joyful thanks to the Father." This is the capstone. The life that pleases God is a thankful life. Not thankful because everything is going well, but thankful because you know who God is and what he's done. Thanksgiving isn't a feeling that comes and goes. It's a decision. It's a posture. It's the recognition that everything you have is a gift you don't deserve, and the God who gave it to you is trustworthy.

RESCUED FROM DARKNESS

Paul's prayer builds to a climax in the final verses, where he zooms out to the enormous thing God has done for them. "Giving joyful thanks to the Father, who has qualified you to share in the inheritance of his holy people in the kingdom of light."

In the Old Testament, each Israelite tribe received a portion of the Promised Land as their inheritance. But Paul transforms that idea. The inheritance for God's people is no longer a piece of land. It's something far greater: a share in the "kingdom of light," a place in God's eternal family.

And the most amazing part? God himself has "qualified" you for this. You didn't earn your spot. You didn't pass a test. God did the qualifying. He looked at people who had no right to be part of his family and said, "I'm making you worthy." That's grace.

Then the language gets dramatic. "For he has rescued us from the dominion of darkness and brought us into the kingdom of the Son he loves, in whom we have redemption, the forgiveness of sins."

This is rescue language. Just as God once rescued the Israelites from slavery in Egypt, he has now rescued his people from something even worse: the dominion of darkness. That phrase refers to the entire system of sin, death, and evil that holds the human race captive. Before the gospel, every person was trapped in that kingdom, whether they realized it or not. Darkness was the address. It was the zip code.

But God didn't leave us there. He "rescued" us and "brought us into the kingdom of the Son he loves." Notice the tenderness of that phrase. This isn't a distant, abstract Son. This is the

Son the Father cherishes and adores. And the kingdom that belongs to this beloved Son is where God's people now live. We've been transferred. We've changed kingdoms.

And in this new kingdom, "we have redemption, the forgiveness of sins." Redemption means being bought out of slavery. That's what Jesus did. He paid the price with his own life to set us free from sin. The result is forgiveness, the complete wiping away of every wrong thing we've ever done. Not because we deserved it. Because God is gracious.

This is where Paul wants the Colossians to stand before he says anything else. You were in darkness, and God brought you into light. You were slaves, and God set you free. You were guilty, and God forgave you.

That's the gospel. That's the foundation.

WHAT THIS MEANS FOR US

First, prayer is one of the most powerful things you can do for someone. Paul was in prison. He couldn't visit the Colossians, couldn't teach them in person, couldn't solve their problems for them. But he could pray. And he did, every single day. If you have friends or family members going through hard times, don't underestimate what your prayers can do. You might not be able to fix their situation, but you can bring their name before the God who can.

Second, knowing God should change how you live. Paul didn't pray for the Colossians to get smarter just for the sake of being smart. He prayed for them to know God so deeply that it transformed everything about how they lived. Real knowledge of God doesn't stay in your head. It travels down into your heart and then out through your hands and feet. If you're learning about God but it's not changing how you treat people, something is off.

Third, you belong to the kingdom of light. If you are in Christ, you have been rescued. You are not stuck in darkness anymore. You are not defined by your worst moments, your biggest failures, or the things other people say about you. God has transferred you into the kingdom of his beloved Son, and that is your new address. When the world feels dark and hopeless, remember where you live now. Remember who brought you there.

Fourth, the gospel is a seed that keeps growing. The same gospel that changed lives in first-century Colossae is still changing lives today. It's the same message, the same power, the same grace. And just as it bore fruit in an overlooked town in ancient Turkey, it can bear fruit in your school, your home, your neighborhood. Don't underestimate the gospel. It's still growing.

TALKING POINTS

1. **Paul prayed for the Colossians even though he had never met them.** Who are some people you could commit to praying for regularly, even if you don't know them well? What would you pray for them?

2. **Paul says the Colossians' faith and love grew out of their "hope stored up in heaven."** How does knowing that your future is secure with God change the way you live right now? Does it make it easier to be generous, brave, or patient? Why or why not?

3. **Paul describes God "rescuing" his people from the "dominion of darkness."** What are some forms of "darkness" that people your age face today? How does the gospel offer rescue from those things?

4. **Epaphras was a faithful but relatively unknown servant of God. He wasn't an apostle or a famous leader, but Paul praised him as "dear" and "faithful."** What does his example teach us about what God values in his people? Would you rather be famous or faithful? Why?

5. **Paul prays for the Colossians to have "great endurance and patience."** Why do you think he specifically prays for those qualities instead of something like success or happiness? When have you needed endurance or patience in your own life?

Paul has laid the foundation. He's reminded the Colossians of where they came from, what God has done for them, and who they are now. But he isn't finished. Because next, he's going to tell them who Jesus really is. Not just a teacher. Not just a miracle worker. Not just a good man who died a noble death. Jesus is something far bigger than any of them had imagined.

Turn the page.

2

BIGGER THAN YOU THINK

Have you ever seen the movie *The Lego Movie*? At the beginning of the story, Emmet Brickowski is the most ordinary person in the entire Lego universe. He follows the instructions. He drinks overpriced coffee. He watches the same show as everybody else. Nobody notices him. Nobody remembers his name. He's about as unremarkable as a person can be.

But then Emmet stumbles onto an ancient relic called the Piece of Resistance, and suddenly everything changes. A mysterious woman named Wyldstyle tells him something unbelievable: there is a prophecy about a "Special" who will save the entire Lego world from Lord Business' plan to glue everything into permanent order. And according to the prophecy, Emmet is the Special.

Here's what makes the movie so fun: for most of the story, Emmet doesn't seem "special" at all. He can't do anything the Master Builders can do. He has no special skills. He's not strong or clever or creative. And everyone around him keeps questioning whether he's really the one the prophecy was talking about.

But by the end of the film, you discover something wild. The Lego world isn't what you thought it was. The camera pulls back, and you realize that the entire story has been taking place on a table in a man's basement. What seemed like a small, self-contained universe turns out to be part of something unimaginably bigger. The scope of the story explodes outward, and everything you thought you knew gets reframed.

That's a little bit like what happens in Colossians 1:15–23.

In chapter one, Paul thanked God for the Colossians' faith, love, and hope. He told them about their rescue from darkness and their transfer into the kingdom of God's beloved Son. That was already amazing. But now Paul pulls the camera back. Way back. He's about to show the Colossians that the Jesus they follow is not just a teacher, not just a healer, not just a man who died and rose again. Jesus is the one through whom everything that exists was created. He holds the entire universe together. He is supreme over every power, every authority, every force in heaven and on earth.

The Colossians thought they knew who Jesus was. They were about to discover he was bigger than they ever imagined.

A HYMN ABOUT JESUS

Scholars have long noticed that Colossians 1:15–20 reads differently from the rest of Paul's letter. The sentences are shorter. The language is more rhythmic. Ideas are stated in careful parallel, almost like poetry. Many believe this section is an early Christian hymn, a song the church may have already known and sung in worship. Whether Paul wrote it himself or borrowed it from the tradition of the early church, one thing is clear: these six verses are among the most stunning statements about Jesus in the entire Bible.

The hymn has two halves, and they mirror each other. The first half is about Jesus and creation. The second half is about Jesus and the new creation, the church. Both halves make the same basic point: Jesus is supreme. He's first. He's over everything. There is nothing in the universe that exists apart from him, and there is nothing in God's rescue plan that works apart from him.

Let's walk through it.

THE IMAGE AND THE FIRSTBORN

"The Son is the image of the invisible God, the firstborn over all creation." Two titles in one sentence. Both are packed with meaning.

First, Jesus is "the image of the invisible God." Nobody has ever seen God. That's a consistent teaching throughout the Bible. God is spirit. He doesn't have a body you can photograph or a face you can sketch. He is, as Paul says here, *invisible*. So how do you know what an invisible God is like?

You look at Jesus.

"Image" doesn't mean a rough copy or a blurry reflection. It means a perfect representation, the way a king's face on a coin represents the king himself. When you see Jesus, you see exactly what God is like. His kindness, his authority, his love, his justice, his mercy. Everything the Father is, Jesus reveals. As one of Jesus' own followers would later write, "No one has ever seen God, but the one and only Son has made him known" (John 1:18).

Second, Jesus is "the firstborn over all creation." This does not mean Jesus was the first thing God created. That would contradict what Paul says in the very next verse. "Firstborn" is a title of rank, not a statement about when someone was born. In the Old Testament, the "firstborn" was the son who held the highest position in the family, the one who received the greatest inheritance and authority. God called Israel his "firstborn" among the nations. He called King David his "firstborn" among the kings of the earth. Neither one was literally the first to exist. Both held the position of highest honor.

That's what Paul is saying about Jesus. He holds the supreme position over everything that has ever been created. He ranks above it all, not because he's part of creation, but because he's the Lord of it.

ALL THINGS CREATED THROUGH HIM

"For in him all things were created: things in heaven and on earth, visible and invisible, whether thrones or powers or rulers or authorities; all things have been created through him and for him."

Read that slowly. Let it sink in.

Everything that exists was created in Jesus, through Jesus, and for Jesus. Not some things. Not most things. *All* things. The stars you see at night. The ground beneath your feet. The air in your lungs. The atoms that hold your body together. Every mountain, every ocean, every galaxy spinning in the darkness of space. All of it was made through him and for him.

But Paul doesn't stop with the physical world. He lists things "visible and invisible," and then he names a category you might not expect: "thrones, powers, rulers, authorities." In the ancient world, people believed the universe was populated with spiritual beings, invisible forces that operated behind the scenes, influencing the world in ways humans couldn't fully see. Some of these beings were good. Some were hostile. And many people in Colossae were afraid of them.

Paul's point is sharp and clear: even those beings were created by Jesus. Whatever spiritual forces exist out there, they owe their existence to him. They are not rivals to Jesus. They are not equal to him. They are his creations. He made them, and he ranks above them.

This mattered enormously for the Colossians, because, as we'll see later in this letter, the false teachers in Colossae were telling Christians they needed to worry about these spiritual powers. They needed special rituals, special rules, and special knowledge to protect themselves. Paul is cutting the legs out from under that argument right here. Why would you be afraid of created beings when you belong to their Creator?

THE ONE WHO HOLDS IT ALL TOGETHER

"He is before all things, and in him all things hold together." The first part is a statement about time: Jesus existed before anything else. Before the earth was formed. Before the stars were lit. Before the first atom came into being. He was already there.

The second part is even more remarkable. Jesus isn't just the one who started the universe. He's the one who keeps it running. "In him all things hold together." The universe isn't a machine that God wound up and walked away from. It's a reality that holds together moment by moment because of Jesus. Without him, everything would fly apart. The laws of physics work because he sustains them. The seasons change because he maintains them. Your heart beats because he upholds it.

This is a Jesus who is far bigger than many people realize. He's not just a figure from ancient history. He's not just a moral teacher whose words are nice to read. He is the reason anything exists at all, and he is the reason it all keeps going.

HEAD OF THE CHURCH, FIRSTBORN FROM THE DEAD

Now the hymn pivots. The focus shifts from creation to the new creation: the church. "And he is the head of the body, the church; he is the beginning and the firstborn from among the dead, so that in everything he might have the supremacy."

Paul uses a powerful image here: the church as a body, with Jesus as the head. In a human body, the head directs everything. It sends signals to the limbs, controls the organs, coordinates all the parts into a unified whole. Without the head, the body can't function.

That's what Jesus is to the church. He's not just the founder. He's not just the example. He's the living head who directs, guides, and gives life to every part of his people. The church doesn't run itself. It runs because Jesus runs it.

Then Paul calls Jesus "the beginning and the firstborn from among the dead." This is the resurrection. Jesus is the first person to pass through death and come out alive on the other side, never to die again. And just as "firstborn" earlier meant supreme rank over creation, "firstborn from among the dead" means Jesus is the first and greatest in a whole new order of existence. He's the pioneer. He went through death first, and everyone who belongs to him will follow.

The purpose of all this? "So that in everything he might have the supremacy." In everything. Not just in religion. Not just in church. Not just in "spiritual" matters. In *everything*. In creation and in the new creation. In the physical world and in the spiritual world. In history and in eternity. There is no category, no realm, no corner of existence where Jesus does not hold the highest place.

ALL THE FULLNESS OF GOD

"For God was pleased to have all his fullness dwell in him, and through him to reconcile to himself all things, whether things on earth or things in heaven, by making peace through his blood, shed on the cross."

This is the climax of the hymn, and it's breathtaking.

"All his fullness." Everything that God is—all of his power, all of his wisdom, all of his love, all of his glory—dwells in Jesus. Not partially. Not in fragments. All of it. If you want to know what God is really like, you don't look at the stars (though they're impressive). You don't read a philosophy book (though some are helpful). You look at Jesus. All the fullness of God lives in him.

And what did this all-powerful, fully divine Jesus do? He reconciled all things to God. "Reconcile" means to bring enemies back together, to restore a broken relationship, to make peace where there was war. The entire creation had been fractured by sin. Humanity was alienated from God. The world itself was groaning under the weight of the fall. And Jesus, through his death on the cross, made peace.

Notice how Paul describes it: "through his blood, shed on the cross." This is not abstract theology. This is a real man, bleeding on a Roman execution device, dying in agony. And yet Paul says this brutal, humiliating death is the moment when peace was made between God and his broken world. The cross looks like defeat, but it's actually the greatest victory in the history of the universe. Through it, God has begun to set everything right.

ONCE ENEMIES, NOW RECONCILED

After the soaring heights of the hymn, Paul brings the camera back down to eye level. He looks directly at the Colossians and says: this cosmic reconciliation? It happened to you.

"Once you were alienated from God and were enemies in your minds because of your evil behavior. But now he has reconciled you by Christ's physical body through death to present you holy in his sight, without blemish and free from accusation."

The Colossians had lived their whole lives in spiritual darkness. Their minds had been turned against God. Their behavior reflected that hostility. They were enemies, not friends.

But now everything is different. God has reconciled them through the physical body of Jesus, through his actual death on a real cross. And the goal of that reconciliation is stunning: to present them "holy, without blemish, and free from accusation." That's the language of a priest examining a sacrifice at the temple, checking it for any defect. God's plan is to present his people before himself as completely pure, with no stain and no charge against them. That's how thorough the work of Christ is. He doesn't just forgive you. He makes you presentable before the holy God of the universe.

But then Paul adds a condition, and it's important.

"If you continue in your faith, established and firm, and do not move from the hope held out in the gospel."

This isn't Paul expressing doubt about whether they're really saved. It's Paul urging them to keep going. Don't drift. Don't wander. Don't let the false teachers pull you away from the gospel that rescued you. Stay rooted. Stay firm. The hope you heard about when Epaphras first told you the good news is real, and it's worth holding onto.

Paul finishes by reminding them of the gospel's reach: "This is the gospel that you heard and that has been proclaimed to every creature under heaven, and of which I, Paul, have become a servant."

The same gospel that reached the Colossians in their little city is the same gospel being announced across the entire world. And Paul, chained in a Roman prison, is its servant. Not its master. Its servant. The greatest apostle in history describes himself as a servant of the message, not the other way around.

WHAT THIS MEANS FOR US

First, Jesus is bigger than you think. It's easy to shrink Jesus down to fit our expectations. We turn him into a nice teacher, a moral example, or a comforting presence when things get hard. All of those things are true, but they're not the whole picture. The Jesus of Colossians 1 is the Creator and Sustainer of the universe, the one in whom all the fullness of God dwells.

When you pray, you're talking to the one who holds galaxies together. Let that reshape how you think about him.

Second, nothing in your life is outside his authority. "In everything he might have the supremacy." That includes your school, your friendships, your family, your struggles, and your future. There is no area of your life where Jesus says, "That's not my department." He is Lord of all of it. When life feels out of control, remember who's holding it together.

Third, reconciliation cost God everything. Peace between God and humanity didn't happen through a magic word or a wave of the hand. It happened through blood. Through a cross. Through the death of God's own Son. If you ever wonder whether God really loves you, look at the cross. That's your answer.

Fourth, keep going. Paul's warning to the Colossians applies to us too: don't move from the hope held out in the gospel. You will face people and ideas that try to pull you away from Jesus, that tell you he's not enough, that you need something more or something different. Don't believe it. Stay rooted. Stay firm. The gospel that saved you is still the truest thing in the universe.

TALKING POINTS

1. **Paul says Jesus is "the image of the invisible God."** What does that tell us about how we can know what God is like? How does looking at Jesus' life help us understand God's character?

2. **Paul says "in him all things hold together."** What do you think it means that Jesus is actively sustaining the universe

right now? How does that change the way you think about ordinary things like gravity, weather, or even your own heartbeat?

3. **The Colossians were tempted to think they needed something more than Jesus for spiritual protection and growth.** What are some things people today add to Jesus, thinking he's not enough on his own?

4. **Paul says that through the cross, God is reconciling "all things" to himself.** What do you think it means for all of creation to be reconciled, not just people? How does that affect the way you think about the world around you?

5. **Paul urges the Colossians to "continue in your faith, established and firm."** What are some practical ways you can stay rooted in the gospel when you face pressure to drift away from it?

Paul has shown the Colossians who Jesus really is: the Creator of everything, the head of the church, the one in whom all of God's fullness lives. But now he needs to tell them something else. He needs to tell them about his own role in God's plan, and why a man sitting in a prison cell is working harder than anyone to bring this message to people he's never met.

Turn the page.

3

SUFFERING ON PURPOSE

If you've seen *National Treasure*, you know that Ben Gates is not a normal person. His entire family has spent generations chasing a legend: a massive treasure hidden by the Founding Fathers of the United States, so enormous that no single person could ever spend it. Ben's grandfather told him about it when he was a kid. His father thinks the whole thing is a waste of time. Historians laugh at him. The FBI ends up chasing him. At one point, he steals the Declaration of Independence.

Ben loses his reputation. He loses his freedom. He risks prison, his friendships, and his life. And he does all of it because he is absolutely convinced that the treasure is real, that it's bigger than anyone imagines, and that finding it is worth whatever it costs him.

Here's the thing: Ben turns out to be right. The treasure exists. And when he finally finds it, hidden in a vast underground chamber beneath a church, it's not just a pile of gold coins. It's an entire room stretching as far as the eye can see, filled with artifacts and riches from civilizations across human history. It's so much bigger than anyone expected that even Ben stands there speechless.

That's not a bad picture of what Paul describes in Colossians 1:24–2:5. Paul has been entrusted with a treasure. Not gold or artifacts, but something far more valuable: the mystery of God's plan for the world, hidden for ages and now finally revealed. And like Ben Gates, Paul has lost everything for it. He's in prison. He's suffered rejection, beatings, and hardship for years. His body bears the scars of his mission.

But Paul isn't complaining. He's rejoicing. Because he knows the treasure is real. He's seen it. And it's bigger than anyone imagined. The mystery he's been entrusted with is nothing less than "Christ in you, the hope of glory." And sharing that treasure with people who need it, even people he's never met, is worth every chain and every scar.

REJOICING IN CHAINS

"Now I rejoice in what I am suffering for you, and I fill up in my flesh what is still lacking in regard to Christ's afflictions, for the sake of his body, which is the church."

That is one of the most startling sentences Paul ever wrote.

Let's start with the obvious part. Paul is suffering. He's in prison. He can't go where he wants. He can't see the people he loves. He's enduring the daily grind of chains, confinement, uncertainty, and the constant threat of execution. And he says he *rejoices* in it.

That's not normal. Most of us would complain. Most of us would ask God why this was happening to us. Paul says he's happy about it.

Why? Because his suffering is "for you." It's for the Colossians. It's for the church. Paul understood that his imprisonment wasn't a random tragedy. It was the cost of his mission. He was in chains precisely because he had spent his life telling everyone he met about Jesus. His suffering wasn't meaningless. It was the price tag on his calling.

But then Paul says something that has puzzled Bible readers for two thousand years: "I fill up in my flesh what is still lacking in regard to Christ's afflictions."

Wait. Is Paul saying that the cross wasn't enough? That Jesus's suffering was incomplete and Paul needs to finish the job?

No. Absolutely not. Paul has already made it crystal clear in this very letter that the cross accomplished everything needed for salvation. Through his blood, God reconciled all things. Nothing is missing from Christ's saving work.

So what does Paul mean?

Think of it this way. When Jesus died and rose again, he defeated sin and death once and for all. That part is finished. But the work of bringing that good news to the world is not finished. And that work involves suffering. Every time a Christian faces rejection for telling someone about Jesus, every time a preacher is thrown in prison, every time a believer endures hardship because of their faith, they are sharing in the kind of suffering that Christ himself experienced. Not adding to his sacrifice, but participating in the ongoing cost of spreading his message.

Paul saw himself as part of a larger story. The gospel had to reach the whole world, and getting it there would involve pain, rejection, and hardship. Paul was absorbing some of that pain on behalf of the church. By drawing the enemy's fire onto himself, he was in some sense shielding the younger churches from attacks they might not yet be strong enough to handle. His suffering served a purpose. It was suffering with a mission.

And that's why he could rejoice.

THE MYSTERY REVEALED

"I have become its servant by the commission God gave me to present to you the word of God in its fullness." Paul didn't choose this career. God chose it for him. The word Paul uses here can be translated "stewardship" or "commission." It's the idea of someone being entrusted with a task by a higher authority. A steward doesn't own the house. He manages it on behalf of the owner. Paul didn't own the gospel. God entrusted it to him and told him to deliver it faithfully.

And what was Paul commissioned to deliver? "The word of God in its fullness." Not a partial message. Not a watered-down version. The full, complete, nothing-left-out truth about what God has done in Christ. This matters enormously in the context of Colossians, because the false teachers in Colossae were apparently offering the Colossians "more." More rules. More spiritual experiences. More secret knowledge. Paul's response is devastating: you already have the full message. What I brought you is complete. You don't need supplements.

Then Paul defines what this "word of God" actually is. "The mystery that has been kept hidden for ages and generations, but is now disclosed to the Lord's people."

In the Bible, a "mystery" isn't a puzzle you solve with clues. It's a secret plan that God kept hidden until the right time and then revealed. For centuries, God's people had been waiting. They knew God had a plan. They could see hints of it in the prophets and the psalms. But the full picture was hidden, like a gift wrapped and placed under the tree weeks before Christmas. You knew something was in there, but you couldn't see what it was until the wrapping came off.

Now the wrapping is off. God has revealed his secret, and it's not a set of rules or a spiritual formula. It's a person.

"To them God has chosen to make known among the Gentiles the glorious riches of this mystery, which is Christ in you, the hope of glory."

There it is. The mystery is Christ. And not just Christ out there somewhere in the universe, reigning over creation from a distance. Christ *in you*. Living inside his people by his Spirit. Present with them. United to them. Inseparable from them.

And this mystery has been made known "among the Gentiles." That would have been shocking to many first-century Jewish ears. The idea that the God of Israel would not only include non-Jewish people in his plan, but would actually dwell inside them by his Spirit? That was the most unexpected twist in the entire story of redemption. God's secret plan wasn't just bigger than anyone expected. It included people nobody expected.

"Christ in you" is also described as "the hope of glory." Because Christ lives in you, your future is secure. The glory that belongs to Christ will one day belong to you too. Not because you earned it, but because you are united to the one who has it. You share in his inheritance because you share in his life. That's the mystery. That's the treasure. That's the whole point.

FULLY MATURE IN CHRIST

"He is the one we proclaim, admonishing and teaching everyone with all wisdom, so that we may present everyone fully mature in Christ." Paul now describes what his ministry actually looks like on a daily basis. He "proclaims" Christ. That's the core of everything he does. Not a philosophy. Not a system of ethics. Not a religious program. A person. Jesus Christ is the content of Paul's preaching.

But proclaiming Christ involves two specific activities. First, "admonishing." This means warning people when they're heading in the wrong direction, straightening out confusion, correcting errors. It's not angry or harsh. It's the kind of honest correction that a good teacher gives a student who is making a mistake. Second, "teaching." This is the positive side, laying out the truth clearly so that people can understand it and live by it.

Notice a word that keeps repeating in this verse: "everyone." Paul proclaims Christ, admonishing *everyone* and teaching *everyone* with all wisdom, so that he may present *everyone* fully mature in Christ. Three times in one sentence. Paul isn't interested in an exclusive club. He isn't saving the best stuff for a select few who have earned access to secret knowledge. The gospel is for everyone, and Paul's goal is to see every single person he encounters grow to full maturity in Christ.

That word "mature" is important. Paul's goal isn't just conversion. It isn't enough for people to simply believe in Jesus and then stay exactly where they are. He wants them to grow up. He wants them to become complete, fully developed followers of Jesus whose lives reflect his character in every area.

He wants them to think differently, love differently, and live differently because Christ is in them.

That's the finish line Paul is running toward. Not fame. Not a comfortable retirement. Mature Christians. People who look like Jesus.

CHRIST'S ENERGY AT WORK

"To this end I strenuously contend with all the energy Christ so powerfully works in me."

Here's the beautiful paradox of Paul's ministry. On the one hand, Paul works incredibly hard. The word he uses here means to labor to the point of exhaustion, like an athlete pushing through the final stretch of a race. Paul isn't casual about his calling. He pours everything he has into it.

But on the other hand, the energy behind all that hard work isn't his own. It's Christ's energy "powerfully at work" in him. Paul sweats and strains, but the power fueling the effort comes from Jesus. It's like a sailboat: the sailor works the ropes and adjusts the sails, but the wind does the real work. Without the wind, the boat goes nowhere.

This is one of the great secrets of the Christian life. God calls you to work hard, but he also provides the power to do it. You don't just grit your teeth and try your best. You lean into the strength that Christ provides. When Paul was exhausted, Christ's power kept him going. When Paul was weak, Christ's energy surged through him. The work was real. The effort was real. But the source was supernatural.

ALL THE TREASURES OF WISDOM AND KNOWLEDGE

"I want you to know how hard I am contending for you and for those at Laodicea, and for all who have not met me personally."

Now Paul gets specific. He's not just working for churches he's visited. He's working for the Colossians, whom he has never met face to face. He's working for the believers in nearby Laodicea. He's working for every Christian who has never shaken his hand or heard his voice in person. His love and labor extend beyond personal relationships into a deep, Spirit-driven concern for people he knows only by report.

Paul tells them what he's working toward: "My goal is that they may be encouraged in heart and united in love, so that they may have the full riches of complete understanding, in order that they may know the mystery of God, namely, Christ, in whom are hidden all the treasures of wisdom and knowledge."

Read that last phrase again: "in whom are hidden all the treasures of wisdom and knowledge." All the treasures. Not some of them. Not the beginner-level treasures with better ones locked behind a paywall. *All* of them. Every scrap of wisdom you could ever need. Every piece of knowledge that matters. It's all stored up in Christ, waiting to be discovered.

This is Paul's direct answer to the false teachers, even though he hasn't named them yet. Whatever they were offering the Colossians, however impressive their arguments or exotic their practices, Paul says it's all unnecessary. Christ already has everything. If you have Christ, you have access to every treasure of wisdom and knowledge that exists. Looking elsewhere is like leaving a palace full of gold to dig in a sandbox.

Paul's concern for the Colossians is both intellectual and relational. He wants them to have "complete understanding," meaning he wants them to *know* the truth deeply. But he also wants them to be "united in love," because truth and love belong together. A church full of knowledgeable people who don't love each other has missed the point. A church full of loving people who don't understand the truth is vulnerable to every false idea that comes along. Paul wants both.

FINE-SOUNDING ARGUMENTS

"I tell you this so that no one may deceive you by fine-sounding arguments. For though I am absent from you in body, I am present with you in spirit and delight to see how disciplined you are and how firm your faith in Christ is."

And here it is. The first direct warning about the false teaching that Paul has been building toward since the beginning of the letter. "I tell you this so that no one may deceive you." Everything Paul has said up to this point—the hymn about Christ's supremacy, the description of the mystery, the emphasis on the treasures of wisdom and knowledge in Christ—has been building a wall around the Colossians to protect them from being tricked.

The danger isn't crude or obvious. It's "fine-sounding arguments." Smooth, polished, persuasive talk that *sounds* reasonable but leads people away from the truth. The most dangerous lies are the ones that sound almost true. Paul wants the Colossians to recognize the difference.

But he ends this section with a word of encouragement. Even though he's never been to Colossae, he's with them in spirit. And what he sees encourages him. The Colossians are "disciplined" and "firm." Paul uses language that sounds almost military, like a general inspecting troops before battle. The church is lined up in proper order. Their defenses are solid. Their faith in Christ is holding.

The battle hasn't started yet. The detailed confrontation with the false teaching is coming in the next chapter. But Paul is pleased with what he sees. The Colossians are ready.

WHAT THIS MEANS FOR US

First, suffering for others can be meaningful. Paul didn't enjoy pain for its own sake. But he understood that his suffering had a purpose. It was the cost of his mission. When you face hardship because of your faith—whether that's social pressure, rejection, or something harder—it helps to know that your suffering isn't random. God can use it for the good of others, just as he used Paul's.

Second, Christ is the mystery revealed. For centuries, God's plan was hidden. Now it's out in the open, and it's not a complicated system or a list of requirements. It's a person. If your faith ever starts to feel like a heavy burden of rules and obligations, come back to this: the heart of Christianity is knowing Christ and being known by him. Everything else flows from that.

Third, all the treasures of wisdom and knowledge are in Christ. You don't need to go looking somewhere else for the answers to life's biggest questions. You don't need a secret formula, a special experience, or a guru with hidden knowledge. Everything you need is found in Jesus. When people try to sell you something "extra," remember what Paul said: the treasures are already yours in Christ.

Fourth, hard work and God's power go together. Paul didn't sit around waiting for God to do everything. He worked himself to exhaustion. But he also knew that the energy behind his work came from Christ. This is the model for your life too. Work hard at whatever God calls you to do, but trust that his power is what makes it count.

TALKING POINTS

1. **Paul said he "rejoiced" in his sufferings.** How is it possible to be joyful while going through something painful? Have you ever experienced something hard that turned out to have a purpose you didn't see at first?

2. **Paul describes the "mystery" of God as "Christ in you, the hope of glory."** What do you think it means for Christ to live inside you? How should that change the way you see yourself?

3. **Paul's goal was to "present everyone fully mature in Christ."** What do you think spiritual maturity looks like for someone your age? How is it different from just knowing facts about the Bible?

4. **Paul warns about "fine-sounding arguments" that can deceive people.** What are some ideas or messages in today's culture that sound good on the surface but might pull people away from the truth of the gospel?

5. **Paul worked extremely hard, but said the energy came from Christ working in him.** How do you balance working hard and trusting God? Can you think of a time when you felt God's strength helping you do something difficult?

Paul has laid his cards on the table. He's told the Colossians who Jesus really is, what the mystery of God contains, and why his own suffering on their behalf makes sense. Now he's ready to do what he's been building toward since the first verse. He's about to confront the false teaching directly, and he's going to dismantle it piece by piece.

Turn the page.

4

DON'T BE FOOLED

If you've seen *Willy Wonka & the Chocolate Factory*, you know what happens to the children who wanted more.

Augustus Gloop wanted more chocolate. He couldn't resist the chocolate river, leaned in too far, and got sucked up a pipe. Violet Beauregarde wanted more gum. She grabbed the experimental piece Wonka warned her not to chew and swelled up into a giant blueberry. Veruca Salt wanted more of everything. She demanded one of Wonka's golden-egg-laying geese, threw a tantrum when she didn't get it, and ended up falling down the garbage chute. Mike Teavee wanted more television. He jumped into Wonka's teleportation machine and got shrunk down to a few inches tall.

Every one of them already had something incredible. They had a golden ticket. They were inside the most extraordinary chocolate factory in the world, surrounded by wonders nobody else had ever seen. But none of that was enough. They each wanted something extra, something beyond what they'd been given, and that grasping for more is exactly what ruined them.

And then there was Charlie. Quiet, patient, grateful Charlie, who didn't grab for anything he wasn't offered. At the end of the story, Wonka turns to him and says he's won the whole factory. Not because Charlie was the smartest or the most talented, but because he was the one who didn't demand more than what he'd been given. He was content to trust Wonka.

That's essentially what Paul tells the Colossians in this chapter. You already have everything you need in Christ. Don't let anyone convince you that you need something more, something flashier, something extra. The false teachers in Colossae were like Augustus, Violet, Veruca, and Mike, grasping for things beyond what God had already provided and leading others to do the same. Paul is about to expose the whole charade.

KEEP WALKING

"So then, just as you received Christ Jesus as Lord, continue to live your lives in him, rooted and built up in him, strengthened in the faith as you were taught, and overflowing with thankfulness."

Before Paul confronts the false teaching, he gives the Colossians a positive command. Keep doing what you're already doing. You received Christ Jesus as Lord. That happened when you first heard the gospel from Epaphras, believed it, and were baptized. That moment was real. That foundation is solid. Now keep walking in that same direction.

Paul stacks up four images to describe what this ongoing life looks like. "Rooted" is a farming/botanical image: like a tree with deep roots that can't be blown over by a storm. "Built up" is a construction image: like a house being assembled on a strong foundation, brick by brick. "Strengthened in the faith" is the idea of growing more firm and stable over time. And "overflowing with thankfulness" is the attitude that should mark everything. When you truly understand what God has done for you, gratitude isn't something you have to force. It overflows naturally.

Notice that Paul doesn't tell them to go looking for something new. He tells them *to go deeper into what they already have*. The Christian life isn't about constantly chasing the next spiritual experience. It's about sinking your roots deeper and deeper into Christ.

THE HOLLOW PHILOSOPHY

"See to it that no one takes you captive through hollow and deceptive philosophy, which depends on human tradition and the elemental spiritual forces of this world rather than on Christ."

Now the gloves come off. Paul names the threat directly: someone is trying to take the Colossians "captive." That's a strong word. It means to carry someone off as a prisoner of war. Paul pictures the false teachers as kidnappers dragging Christians away from Christ's family and locking them up in a lesser system.

What is this dangerous teaching? Paul calls it a "philosophy," but he doesn't mean the kind of philosophy you study in school. In the ancient world, many religious systems called themselves philosophies. This particular one was "hollow and deceptive." It looked impressive on the outside but had nothing of real value on the inside, like a beautifully wrapped gift box with nothing in it.

Paul says this philosophy "depends on human tradition and the elemental spiritual forces of this world rather than on Christ." Scholars have debated for centuries exactly what Paul meant by "elemental spiritual forces." The phrase could refer to basic spiritual principles that governed the old way of life, or to spiritual beings that people believed controlled the universe. Either way, the point is the same: this teaching was rooted in the old world, the world that existed before Christ came and changed everything. It was offering the Colossians something that belonged to the past, not the future.

And here's the core of the problem: it depended on something "rather than on Christ." Whatever it added, whatever it required, it was pulling people away from the one thing that actually mattered. Anything that replaces Christ or supplements Christ as the center of your faith is, by definition, a step backward.

ALREADY COMPLETE

"For in Christ all the fullness of the Deity lives in bodily form, and in Christ you have been brought to fullness. He is the head over every power and authority."

Paul has already said something like this in 1:19, but now he sharpens it. All the fullness of God lives in Jesus—not in pieces or fragments but completely—in "bodily form." The invisible God has made himself fully present in an actual human being. Everything you could ever want to know about God, everything you could ever need from God, is available in Jesus.

And then the knockout punch: "in Christ you have been brought to fullness." You're already full. You're already complete. You don't have anything missing that some other teaching needs to supply. If all the fullness of God lives in Christ, and you are in Christ, then you already have access to everything God offers.

Why would you go looking for spiritual supplements when you're already connected to the source of all spiritual reality?

Paul adds that Christ "is the head over every power and authority." Whatever spiritual forces the false teachers were worried about, whatever invisible powers they claimed Christians needed to appease or fear, Christ rules over every one of them. He made them. He outranks them. They answer to him. Being afraid of spiritual powers when you belong to their Creator is like being afraid of the waves when you're standing with the one who made the ocean.

BURIED AND RAISED

"In him you were also circumcised with a circumcision not done by human hands. Your whole self, ruled by the flesh, was put off when you were circumcised by Christ, having been buried with him in baptism, in which you were also raised with him through your faith in the power of God, who raised him from the dead."

This might sound confusing at first, but the basic idea is powerful.

In the Old Testament, circumcision was the physical sign that you belonged to God's people. It was the mark of membership. The false teachers may have been telling the Colossians that they needed to be physically circumcised to be fully part of God's family. Paul says no. You've already received a circumcision, but it's not the kind done with human hands. When you were united to Christ in baptism, something happened to you spiritually. Your old self, the person you were before you knew Christ, was stripped away. You were buried with Christ in the water, and you were raised with him to a new life.

Paul is painting a vivid picture. Baptism is like a funeral and a birth rolled into one. The old you goes down into the water and dies. The new you comes up out of the water alive. And this transformation happened through "your faith in the power of God, who raised him from the dead." The same power that brought Jesus back from the grave is the power that gave you new life.

If God's resurrection power has already been at work in you, what could any human religious system possibly add?

THE CROSS CHANGES EVERYTHING

"When you were dead in your sins and in the uncircumcision of your flesh, God made you alive with Christ. He forgave us all our sins, having canceled the charge of our legal indebtedness, which stood against us and condemned us; he has taken it away, nailing it to the cross. And having disarmed the powers and authorities, he made a public spectacle of them, triumphing over them by the cross."

This is one of the most dramatic passages Paul ever wrote. He uses three images to describe what happened at the cross, and each one is more vivid than the last.

First, God "forgave all our sins." Before Christ, humanity owed a debt it could never repay. Every wrong thought, every selfish action, every act of rebellion against God added to the bill. It was a debt that grew and grew, with no hope of ever being settled. But God canceled it. He didn't reduce it or restructure it. He wiped it clean. And the way he did it was by nailing it to the cross. In the ancient world, when a criminal was crucified, a notice listing their crimes was posted above their head. Paul pictures God taking the record of our sins and nailing it to Christ's cross, as if Jesus himself were guilty of all of it. He took our debt and paid it with his life.

Second, God "disarmed the powers and authorities." Whatever spiritual forces had been holding humanity captive, whatever powers had been using sin and law and fear to keep people enslaved, the cross stripped them of their weapons. They're powerless now. They've been neutralized.

Third, God "made a public spectacle of them, triumphing over them by the cross." This is the language of a Roman victory parade. When a Roman general conquered an enemy, he would march through the streets of Rome with the defeated soldiers chained behind him for everyone to see. Paul says God did exactly that to the spiritual powers at the cross. What looked like the darkest moment in history, the execution of God's Son, was actually the greatest victory ever won. The cross didn't just save individuals. It defeated the forces of evil themselves.

SHADOWS AND SUBSTANCE

"Therefore do not let anyone judge you by what you eat or drink, or with regard to a religious festival, a New Moon celebration or a Sabbath day. These are a shadow of the things that were to come; the reality, however, is found in Christ."

Now Paul applies all of this to the specific demands the false teachers were making. They were telling the Colossians they needed to follow certain dietary rules, observe certain religious holidays, and keep certain Sabbath regulations. These were all part of the Old Testament law, rules that God had given to Israel for a specific time and a specific purpose.

Paul's response is brilliant. He doesn't say those rules were bad. He says they were shadows. Imagine you're walking toward a building on a sunny day. Before you reach the building, you see its shadow stretching across the ground in front of you. The shadow tells you something real is coming. It gives you a rough idea of the shape. But once you reach the actual building, you don't stand there staring at the shadow anymore. You go inside.

That's what the Old Testament regulations were. They were shadows pointing forward to something real that was coming. And now the real thing has arrived. Christ is the substance. He's the building. Clinging to the old regulations after Christ has come is like choosing the shadow over the thing it was pointing to.

DON'T LET ANYONE DISQUALIFY YOU

"Do not let anyone who delights in false humility and the worship of angels disqualify you. Such a person also goes into great detail about what they have seen; they are puffed up with idle notions by their unspiritual mind. They have lost connection with the head, from whom the whole body, supported and held together by its ligaments and sinews, grows as God causes it to grow."

Paul warns against a second type of false teacher: the kind who claims to have special spiritual experiences, visions of angels, and a deeper level of spirituality than everyone else. These people put on a show of extreme humility and intense piety, but Paul says they are actually "puffed up" with pride. Their impressive spirituality is really just a swollen ego dressed in religious clothing.

The real problem? "They have lost connection with the head." Remember from chapter 2 that Christ is the head of the body, the church. These teachers might look spiritual. They might sound impressive. But they've disconnected themselves from Jesus. And a body disconnected from its head can't grow. It can only wither.

Real spiritual growth doesn't come from chasing visions or following self-appointed spiritual experts. It comes from staying connected to Christ. He's the one who causes the body to grow, holding it together through the relationships and structures he has designed.

RULES CAN'T CHANGE YOUR HEART

"Since you died with Christ to the elemental spiritual forces of this world, why, as though you still belonged to the world, do you submit to its rules: 'Do not handle! Do not taste! Do not touch!'? These rules, which have to do with things that are all destined to perish with use, are based on merely human commands and teachings. Such regulations indeed have an appearance of wisdom, with their self-imposed worship, their false humility and their harsh treatment of the body, but they lack any value in restraining sensual indulgence."

Paul saves his sharpest words for last. He lists the kinds of rules the false teachers were pushing: don't handle this, don't taste that, don't touch this other thing. Strict regulations about what you could eat, what you could touch, how you should treat your body.

And then he says something that must have shocked some of his readers: these rules are useless.

Not useless in the sense that discipline doesn't matter. Paul will have plenty to say about how Christians should live in the next chapter. But useless in the sense that *external rules, by themselves, cannot change your heart.* You can follow every regulation perfectly and still be full of pride, anger, lust, and selfishness on the inside. The rules might make you look spiritual on the outside, but they "lack any value in restraining sensual indulgence." They can control your behavior, but they can't transform your character.

Real transformation doesn't come from the outside in. It comes from the inside out, from being connected to Christ, filled with his Spirit, and growing in genuine knowledge of God. That's what Paul will turn to next.

WHAT THIS MEANS FOR US

First, you are already complete in Christ. You don't need a spiritual upgrade. You don't need secret knowledge, special experiences, or extra rules to be fully accepted by God. If you belong to Jesus, you have everything you need. When someone tells you that Jesus isn't enough, that's the oldest lie in the book.

Second, the cross defeated every enemy. Sin, death, the powers of evil—they have all been disarmed. The victory has already been won. You don't need to live in fear of spiritual forces or unseen powers. Christ has already triumphed over them, and you are in him.

Third, don't trade substance for shadows. It's tempting to measure your spiritual life by external things: how many rules you follow, how often you attend church, what you eat or don't eat. Those things might have their place, but they're not the point. Christ is the point. Stay connected to him, and the rest will follow.

Fourth, rules can't change your heart. Only Christ can do that. If your faith is mostly about what you're not allowed to do, something has gone wrong. The Christian life isn't a list of restrictions. It's a relationship with the living God who is transforming you from the inside out.

TALKING POINTS

1. **In Willy Wonka, the children who grabbed for more than what they'd been given ended up worse off, while Charlie, who was simply grateful, received everything.** How does that parallel what Paul is saying about the Colossians and the false teachers?

2. **Paul says the Colossians are "already complete" in Christ.** Why do you think it's so hard for people to believe that? What makes us feel like we need something more?

3. **Paul describes the Old Testament rules as "shadows" and Christ as the "reality."** Can you think of other examples where a shadow or a preview points to something greater that eventually arrives?

4. **Paul says the false teachers' rules had "an appearance of wisdom" but couldn't actually change people's hearts.**

What's the difference between looking spiritual and actually being transformed by God? How can you tell the difference?

5. **Paul warns against people who claim to have special spiritual experiences and look down on others.** How can you tell the difference between genuine spiritual maturity and spiritual pride?

Paul has dismantled the false teaching piece by piece. He's shown the Colossians that Christ is supreme, that the cross has defeated every rival power, and that no set of human rules can do what Christ has already done. But tearing down the counterfeit isn't enough. The Colossians need to know what the real thing looks like. What does it actually mean to live as someone who has been raised with Christ?

Turn the page.

5

TAKING OFF AND PUTTING ON

Have you ever gone through your closet and realized half the stuff in there doesn't fit anymore? Maybe your parents made you do it. Maybe you did it yourself because you couldn't find anything to wear. Either way, you pulled everything out, held each item up, and asked the same question over and over: Does this still belong here?

Some things were obvious. That shirt from three years ago that barely reaches your belly button? Gone. Those shoes you've been cramming your feet into even though your toes are curled? Gone. That jacket you've kept because you used to love it, even though the zipper is broken and the lining is torn? Time to let it go.

But cleaning out the old stuff is only half the job. The other half is putting on what actually fits. New clothes that match who you are now, not who you were two years ago. Clothes that are the right size, the right style, the right look for this version of you. You're not the same person you were in third grade, and your wardrobe shouldn't pretend you are.

Paul uses exactly this image in Colossians 3. He tells the Colossians that their old life is like a set of worn-out, ill-fitting clothes that need to come off. And their new life in Christ is like a brand-new wardrobe that God has picked out for them. The chapter is organized around two simple commands: take off the old stuff, and put on the new. But what Paul describes isn't a wardrobe makeover. It's a life makeover, the kind that starts deep inside and works its way out into everything you say and do.

SET YOUR MINDS ON THINGS ABOVE

"Since, then, you have been raised with Christ, set your hearts on things above, where Christ is, seated at the right hand of God. Set your minds on things above, not on earthly things. For you died, and your life is now hidden with Christ in God. When Christ, who is your life, appears, then you also will appear with him in glory."

Before Paul gets to the wardrobe, he sets the foundation. Everything that follows is built on this: you have been raised with Christ. In the last chapter, Paul said the Colossians died with Christ in baptism. Now he completes the picture. You didn't just die. You were raised. You came up out of that water into a new life, connected to the risen Jesus.

And because you've been raised with him, Paul says, "set your hearts on things above." Direct your attention, your desires, your ambitions upward, toward the place where Christ is now reigning. This isn't Paul telling you to walk around staring at the sky or to stop caring about your daily life. "Things above" doesn't mean "things that aren't practical."

It means the character of Christ, the values of his kingdom, the kind of life that reflects heaven's priorities rather than the world's priorities.

Paul contrasts "things above" with "earthly things." He's not talking about sports, homework, or hanging out with friends. Those are all normal parts of life. "Earthly things" in this context means the old way of living, the life that belonged to the age before Christ came. The selfishness, the greed, the anger, the lies. Those belong to the old world. They don't fit anymore.

Then Paul says something mysterious and beautiful: "Your life is now hidden with Christ in God." Right now, your true identity as a child of God isn't fully visible to the world. People might not see it. Sometimes you might not even feel it. But it's real, and it's safe, tucked away with Christ in God like a treasure locked in a vault. Nobody can steal it. Nobody can damage it.

And one day it will be revealed. "When Christ, who is your life, appears, then you also will appear with him in glory." When Jesus returns, everything hidden will be uncovered. The world will finally see who you really are: a person made new by God, shining with the glory of Christ himself. That's your future. That's your destiny. And it's the reason Paul says what he says next.

TAKE OFF THE OLD CLOTHES

"Put to death, therefore, whatever belongs to your earthly nature: sexual immorality, impurity, lust, evil desires and greed, which is idolatry. Because of these, the wrath of God is coming. You used to walk in these ways, in the life you once lived."

Paul doesn't ease into this. He says "put to death." Not "gradually reduce." Not "try to manage." Put it to death. Kill it. These things don't belong in your life anymore, and they need to go.

The first list focuses on sins that twist the good gift of physical desire into something selfish and destructive. Sexual immorality, impurity, lust, evil desires. These are all different shades of the same basic problem: wanting something that isn't yours to have and refusing to wait for God's design. Paul traces the progression in reverse, from the general attitude (evil desires) down to the specific action (sexual immorality), showing that sin usually starts as a thought before it becomes a behavior.

Then he names greed, and he calls it something shocking: idolatry. Worship of a false god. Greed takes something good and puts it at the center of your life where only God belongs. When you organize your entire existence around getting more, wanting more, having more, you've built an altar to yourself. That's what idolatry is: putting anything in God's place.

Paul says these are things the Colossians "used to walk in." Past tense. That was the old life. That was who they were before Christ. They need to leave it behind the way you leave behind clothes that no longer fit.

"But now you must also rid yourselves of all such things as these: anger, rage, malice, slander, and filthy language from your lips. Do not lie to each other." The second list shifts from sexual sins to sins of speech and attitude. Anger that simmers. Rage that explodes. Malice that wants to hurt people. Slander that destroys reputations. Filthy language that pollutes conversations. And lying, which poisons every relationship it touches.

Notice something important: Paul puts these sins right next to the sexual sins, as if they're equally serious. Most people would rank them differently. We tend to think of anger and gossip as minor offenses compared to more dramatic sins. But Paul treats them the same way. A church that would never tolerate sexual immorality but is full of backbiting, gossip, and explosive tempers has only cleaned out half the closet.

"Since you have taken off your old self with its practices and have put on the new self, which is being renewed in knowledge in the image of its Creator." Here's the clothing image in full. The "old self" is like a set of clothes you've stripped off and thrown away. The "new self" is what you've put on in its place. And this new self isn't static. It's "being renewed." It's an ongoing process, a daily transformation, as God reshapes you more and more into the image of Christ, the Creator who made you in the first place.

This is the opposite of the false teaching Paul attacked in chapter 2. The false teachers said you need external rules and rituals to become spiritually complete. Paul says God is doing something far deeper. He's remaking you from the inside, restoring the image that was damaged by sin, creating a new kind of human being.

NO MORE WALLS

"Here there is no Gentile or Jew, circumcised or uncircumcised, barbarian, Scythian, slave or free, but Christ is all, and is in all." Paul pauses to make a point that would have rattled his first-century audience. In this new community, the old divisions are gone.

In the ancient world, your identity was largely determined by your ethnicity, your religion, your social class, and your culture. Greeks looked down on Jews. Jews looked down on Gentiles. Everyone looked down on barbarians and Scythians, who were considered barely civilized. And the line between slave and free was absolute. These categories defined who you were, who you could associate with, and how much respect you deserved.

Paul says all of that is irrelevant now. In Christ, those walls have been demolished. It doesn't matter where you come from, what language you speak, what color your skin is, or what your family's bank account looks like. "Christ is all, and is in all." He is the identity that supersedes every other identity. When you look at a fellow Christian, you're not supposed to see their race or their social status first. You're supposed to see someone who belongs to Christ, just like you do.

This doesn't mean differences disappear. People still come from different backgrounds and cultures. But those differences can no longer be used to rank people or exclude them from the family of God. The new self that is "being renewed in the image of its Creator" looks the same regardless of what passport you carry.

PUT ON THE NEW CLOTHES

"Therefore, as God's chosen people, holy and dearly loved, clothe yourselves with compassion, kindness, humility, gentleness and patience." Now comes the beautiful part. After all the "take off" language, Paul switches to "put on." And the clothes he describes are stunning.

Before listing the virtues, Paul reminds the Colossians who they are. They are "God's chosen people, holy and dearly loved." Those three phrases used to describe Israel, God's special nation. Now Paul applies them to the church, this mixed community of Jews and Gentiles who belong to Christ. You are chosen. You are set apart. You are loved. That's your identity. Now dress accordingly.

Compassion is the ability to feel what someone else is feeling, to let their suffering move you deep in your gut. Kindness is compassion in action, treating people with warmth and generosity even when you don't have to. Humility is thinking honestly about yourself, not pretending to be more important than you are, and not needing to be the center of attention. Gentleness is the strength that refuses to be harsh. And patience is the ability to put up with difficult people and difficult circumstances without losing your temper.

"Bear with each other and forgive one another if any of you has a grievance against someone. Forgive as the Lord forgave you." This is where it gets personal. It's easy to talk about compassion and kindness in the abstract. It's much harder when someone has actually wronged you. Paul says bear with each other. That means tolerating the annoying habits and rough edges of the people around you. Nobody is perfect, and community requires a daily decision to extend grace to imperfect people.

And when someone does something worse than annoying—when they actually hurt you—the command is forgive. Not because what they did was okay. Not because you should pretend it didn't happen. But because the Lord forgave you. If God, who had every right to hold your sins against you forever, chose instead to cancel the debt and welcome you into his family, then you have no right to refuse that same grace to someone else.

"And over all these virtues put on love, which binds them all together in perfect unity." Love is the outer garment that holds everything else together. Without love, compassion becomes pity. Kindness becomes performance. Patience becomes passive aggression. Love is the thread that runs through every other virtue and gives it its proper shape. It's the thing that makes all the rest work.

PEACE, GRATITUDE, AND THE WORD OF CHRIST

"Let the peace of Christ rule in your hearts, since as members of one body you were called to peace. And be thankful."

"Peace" here isn't just a feeling of personal calm. It's the peace that exists between people in a healthy community. When disagreements arise, when tensions flare, the peace of Christ is supposed to act like a referee, stepping in to settle the dispute. You were called to this peace when you were brought into one body, the church. Protecting that peace is everyone's responsibility.

And once again, Paul adds: "Be thankful." This is the drumbeat of the entire letter. Gratitude is the atmosphere that everything else is supposed to live in.

"Let the message of Christ dwell among you richly as you teach and admonish one another with all wisdom through psalms, hymns, and songs from the Spirit, singing to God with gratitude in your hearts."

The community Paul envisions isn't one where only the leaders teach. Everyone has a role in building each other up.

The "message of Christ," the gospel truth about who Jesus is and what he has done, should be so deeply embedded in the life of the church that it overflows into teaching, encouragement, correction, and worship. Psalms, hymns, and spiritual songs aren't just for Sunday mornings. They're part of how the community learns, remembers, and celebrates the truth.

"And whatever you do, whether in word or deed, do it all in the name of the Lord Jesus, giving thanks to God the Father through him."

Paul finishes with the widest possible scope. Whatever you do. Not just the "spiritual" stuff. Not just the stuff that happens at church. Whatever you do, in every word and every action, do it as a representative of Jesus. Do it in a way that honors his name. And do it with thanksgiving, because everything you have, everything you are, and everything you will become is a gift from God through Christ.

That's the new wardrobe. That's what it looks like to live as someone who has been raised with Christ.

WHAT THIS MEANS FOR US

First, your identity determines your behavior. Paul doesn't start with rules. He starts with identity: you have been raised with Christ. You are God's chosen people, holy and dearly loved. When you know who you are, the way you live flows naturally from that knowledge. You don't obey God to earn his love. You obey him because you already have it.

Second, sin needs to be dealt with directly. Paul doesn't suggest gradually improving. He says "put to death." That sounds extreme, but sin doesn't respond well to half-measures.

If something in your life is pulling you away from Christ, don't negotiate with it. Cut it off. Ask for help. Be honest about it. The new life requires decisive action against the old one.

Third, how you speak matters as much as how you act. Paul puts anger, slander, and lying in the same list with sexual immorality and greed. Your words have power. They can build people up or tear them down. The way you talk about people when they're not in the room reveals more about your character than almost anything else.

Fourth, forgiveness isn't optional. If you've been forgiven by God, you are expected to forgive others. That doesn't mean pretending it didn't hurt. It means releasing the debt, choosing not to hold it over the person's head, and trusting God to handle the justice.

TALKING POINTS

1. **Paul says to "set your minds on things above."** What do you think that looks like practically in your daily life? How is it different from just thinking about heaven all day?

2. **Paul lists sins of anger and speech alongside sexual sins, treating them as equally serious.** Why do you think we tend to rank some sins as worse than others? Is that ranking accurate?

3. **Paul says in Christ "there is no Gentile or Jew… slave or free."** What are some of the divisions and categories that people use today to rank each other? How should being in Christ change the way we think about those differences?

4. **Paul lists five virtues that should characterize every Christian: compassion, kindness, humility, gentleness, and**

patience. Of these five, which one is hardest for you? Why do you think that is?

5. **Paul says to do "whatever you do" in the name of Jesus.** How would your day look different if you really tried to do everything as a representative of Christ?

Paul has described the new life from the inside out: new thoughts, new attitudes, new speech, new relationships. But what does this look like in the places where you actually spend your time: at home, at work, in the relationships closest to you? That's where Paul turns next, bringing the gospel down to the most ordinary corners of everyday life.

Turn the page.

6

THE GOSPEL AT HOME

Rudyard Kipling's *The Jungle Books* tells the story of Mowgli, a human boy raised by wolves in the jungles of India. Mowgli doesn't just wander through the jungle doing whatever he pleases. From his earliest days in the wolf pack, he has to learn the Law of the Jungle.

The Law of the Jungle isn't about survival of the fittest or the strongest animal getting its way. It's actually a set of rules designed to protect every member of the community. The pack hunts together, shares food, and watches over each other's cubs. Older wolves have responsibilities toward younger ones. Stronger animals have duties toward weaker ones. As Kipling writes, "The strength of the pack is the wolf, and the strength of the wolf is the pack." Every member matters, and every member has a role to play.

When Mowgli breaks the Law, things go badly for him and for everyone around him. When he honors it, the whole community benefits. The Law isn't there to crush him. It's there to hold the pack together, to make sure that freedom doesn't turn into chaos and that strength doesn't become an excuse for cruelty.

That idea, that genuine community requires each member to understand their role and treat each other with care, is exactly what Paul addresses in the final section of Colossians. He brings the soaring theology of the earlier chapters down to the kitchen table. After talking about the supremacy of Christ, the defeat of spiritual powers, and the transformation of the inner self, Paul now asks: What does all of this look like on a Tuesday afternoon? How does the gospel change the way you treat your family? How does it affect the way you work, the way you pray, the way you talk to people who don't share your faith?

The answer, it turns out, is that the gospel touches everything.

LIFE AT HOME

"Wives, submit yourselves to your husbands, as is fitting in the Lord. Husbands, love your wives and do not be harsh with them. Children, obey your parents in everything, for this pleases the Lord. Fathers, do not embitter your children, or they will become discouraged."

This section is what is often called the "household code." In the ancient world, both Jewish and pagan writers produced lists of instructions for how members of a household should relate to one another. Paul does something similar here, but with a crucial difference: every relationship is reshaped by Christ.

Notice the careful balance. Paul doesn't just tell one side what to do. He addresses both sides of each relationship, and he gives each side both responsibilities and protections.

Wives are told to submit to their husbands "as is fitting in the Lord." This doesn't mean wives are inferior or that they should accept mistreatment. The word "submit" describes a voluntary willingness to respect and support the leadership of the household. But immediately, Paul turns to husbands and tells them to "love your wives and do not be harsh with them." A husband who loves his wife the way Christ loves the church would never use his position to bully, control, or belittle her. The two commands work together: mutual respect and sacrificial love create a marriage where both people flourish.

Then Paul addresses children: "Obey your parents in everything, for this pleases the Lord." If you're young, this verse is speaking directly to you. Obeying your parents is one of the most basic and important things you can do as a young follower of Jesus. It's not always easy. Sometimes your parents' rules feel unfair. Sometimes you're convinced you know better. But Paul says obedience in this area pleases God, and that should matter more than whether it makes sense to you in the moment.

But Paul doesn't leave it there. He immediately tells fathers (and the word can include both parents): "Do not embitter your children, or they will become discouraged." This is remarkable. In the ancient world, fathers had almost unlimited authority over their children. Paul puts a check on that authority. Parents are not supposed to crush their children's spirits with constant criticism, impossible expectations, or conditional love. A child who hears nothing but "you're not good enough" will eventually believe it. God wants parents to raise their children the way he treats his own children: with firm boundaries wrapped in deep, unconditional love.

WORK AS WORSHIP

"Slaves, obey your earthly masters in everything; and do it, not only when their eye is on you and to win their favor, but with sincerity of heart and reverence for the Lord. Whatever you do, work at it with all your heart, as working for the Lord, not for human masters, since you know that you will receive an inheritance from the Lord as a reward. It is the Lord Christ you are serving."

We need to pause here and acknowledge something. Paul is writing to a world where slavery was a reality. Millions of people in the Roman Empire were enslaved, and some of them were Christians. Paul does not call for a political revolution against slavery in this letter. But what he does is quietly revolutionary in a different way: he treats slaves as full human beings with dignity, rights, and a direct relationship to God. In a world that considered slaves to be property, that was explosive.

Paul tells enslaved Christians to work with sincerity and wholehearted effort, not because their masters deserve it, but because they are ultimately working for Jesus. "Whatever you do, work at it with all your heart, as working for the Lord." This principle reaches far beyond the ancient world. Whether you're doing homework, cleaning your room, mowing a neighbor's lawn, or working a part-time job, the same truth applies. You're not just working for a teacher, a parent, or a boss. You're working for Christ. That changes everything about how you approach even the most boring or thankless task.

Then Paul addresses masters: "Provide your slaves with what is right and fair, because you know that you also have a Master in heaven." In one sentence, Paul dismantles the idea that power gives you the right to exploit people. Masters have a Master. Authority is always accountable to a higher authority.

If you have any kind of power over another person, God expects you to use it justly.

PRAY, WATCH, AND BE THANKFUL

"Devote yourselves to prayer, being watchful and thankful. And pray for us, too, that God may open a door for our message, so that we may proclaim the mystery of Christ, for which I am in chains. Pray that I may proclaim it clearly, as I should."

Paul now turns from household instructions to the broader Christian life. And the first thing he mentions is prayer. Not as an afterthought. Not as one item on a long list. "Devote yourselves to prayer." Make it a priority. Be consistent. Be serious about it.

He adds two qualities that should mark their prayers: watchfulness and thankfulness. "Watchful" means staying alert, keeping your eyes open for what God is doing and for the needs around you. "Thankful" is the attitude that has echoed through this entire letter. Gratitude is the oxygen of the Christian life.

Then Paul makes a personal request: pray for me. Remember, he's writing from prison. He could ask them to pray for his release, his comfort, or his safety. Instead, he asks them to pray that God would "open a door" for the gospel message. Even in chains, Paul's primary concern isn't his own freedom. It's the mission. He wants to keep proclaiming Christ clearly, even from a prison cell. That's the kind of single-minded devotion that marks a life truly surrendered to God.

WISE TOWARD OUTSIDERS

"Be wise in the way you act toward outsiders; make the most of every opportunity. Let your conversation be always full of grace, seasoned with salt, so that you may know how to answer everyone."

Paul cares about how Christians are perceived by people who don't yet know Christ. "Outsiders" is his term for non-believers, and he wants the Colossians to be thoughtful about how they interact with them.

"Make the most of every opportunity." Every conversation, every encounter, every relationship with a non-Christian is an opportunity to reflect the character of Jesus. That doesn't mean hitting people over the head with a Bible. It means living in a way that makes them curious. It means being the kind of person who makes others wonder, "What's different about them?"

And when the opportunity comes to actually talk about your faith, Paul says your speech should be "full of grace, seasoned with salt." Grace means warmth, kindness, and genuine respect for the other person. Salt means flavor, wit, and substance. Your words should be interesting, not boring. Honest, not preachy. Thoughtful, not rehearsed. Paul wants Christians to be the kind of people others actually enjoy talking to.

THE PEOPLE BEHIND THE LETTER

"Tychicus will tell you all the news about me. He is a dear brother, a faithful minister and fellow servant in the Lord. I am sending him to you for the express purpose that you may know about our circumstances and that he may encourage your hearts. He is coming with Onesimus, our faithful and dear brother, who is one of you. They will tell you everything that is happening here."

In the final section of the letter, Paul introduces and greets a whole cast of characters. These verses might seem like a list of unfamiliar names, but they're actually a window into the real, human community that surrounded Paul and supported his ministry.

Tychicus is the letter carrier, the man physically delivering this scroll to Colossae. Paul calls him a "dear brother, faithful minister, and fellow servant." He's not famous. He's not an apostle. He's a reliable, trustworthy worker who gets the job done. Paul is sending him not just to drop off the mail but to encourage the Colossians with firsthand news.

Traveling with Tychicus is Onesimus, whom Paul calls "our faithful and dear brother, who is one of you." This is the same Onesimus we'll meet in the letter to Philemon. He's a runaway slave from Colossae who met Paul in prison and became a Christian. Now he's going home, and Paul wants the church to welcome him as a brother, not reject him as a fugitive. That simple introduction carries enormous weight.

Paul then passes along greetings from six colleagues. Aristarchus, who is in prison with Paul. Mark, the cousin of Barnabas, who had once deserted Paul on a missionary journey but has clearly been restored (he wrote the Gospel that bears his name). A man named Jesus, also called Justus. Paul notes that these three are his only Jewish coworkers, and they have been "a comfort" to him. Then Epaphras, the man who first brought the gospel to Colossae, who is "always wrestling in prayer" for them. Luke, "the dear doctor," who would later write the Gospel that shares his name and the book of Acts. And Demas, who is with Paul now but who, according to a later letter, would eventually walk away from the faith.

These aren't just names on a page. They're real people with real stories, real struggles, and real faith. Some of them will remain faithful to the end. Some will stumble. All of them are part of the messy, beautiful community that God uses to carry his gospel to the world.

FINAL INSTRUCTIONS

"After this letter has been read to you, see that it is also read in the church of the Laodiceans and that you in turn read the letter from Laodicea."

Paul intends this letter to be shared. It wasn't just for Colossae. The neighboring church in Laodicea was supposed to hear it too, and the Colossians were supposed to read a letter Paul had sent to Laodicea. From the very beginning, Paul's letters were treated as more than personal correspondence. They carried the authority of an apostle, and they were meant to be read aloud in the assembled church, studied, and passed on. That's how the letters that eventually became part of our New Testament first circulated.

Paul also sends a message to a man named Archippus: "See to it that you complete the ministry you have received in the Lord." We don't know exactly what Archippus' assignment was, but Paul wanted him to finish it. The work God gives you matters, and leaving it incomplete is not an option.

Then Paul picks up the pen himself. Throughout the letter, he had been dictating to a secretary, as was common in the ancient world. But for the final line, he writes in his own hand:

"I, Paul, write this greeting in my own hand. Remember my chains. Grace be with you."

Remember my chains. It's a brief, piercing reminder. The man who wrote this extraordinary letter about the supremacy of Christ, the defeat of spiritual powers, the beauty of the new life, and the transformation of every human relationship did so while sitting in a Roman prison. His wrists were bound. His freedom was gone. And yet his final word is not self-pity. It's grace. The same grace that opened the letter now closes it. Everything in between has been an outpouring of that grace, applied to every corner of life.

WHAT THIS MEANS FOR US

First, the gospel belongs at home. It's easy to be a Christian at church and something else entirely at home. Paul says the two can't be separated. How you treat your parents, your siblings, and eventually your spouse is a direct reflection of what you believe about Jesus. The gospel isn't just for Sundays. It's for Tuesday afternoon at the kitchen table.

Second, every task can be an act of worship. "Whatever you do, work at it with all your heart, as working for the Lord." That homework assignment? Do it for Jesus. That chore your parents asked you to do? Do it for Jesus. When you see every task as an offering to God, nothing is meaningless.

Third, how you talk to outsiders matters. People who don't know Jesus are watching how you live and listening to how you speak. Paul says your words should be "full of grace, seasoned with salt." Be kind. Be interesting. Be real. And be ready to explain why you live the way you do.

Fourth, real community is made up of real people. The list of names at the end of Colossians reminds us that the church isn't an institution. It's people. Flawed, faithful, sometimes failing people who show up for each other. That's what God works through.

TALKING POINTS

1. **Paul tells children to obey their parents and tells parents not to embitter their children.** Why do you think he addresses both sides? What does it look like when one side is emphasized and the other is ignored?
2. **Paul says to work "as for the Lord, not for human masters."** How would your attitude toward homework, chores, or other responsibilities change if you truly believed you were doing them for Jesus?
3. **Paul asks the Colossians to pray that God would "open a door" for the gospel.** What doors for the gospel do you see in your own life? Where are the opportunities to share your faith?
4. **Paul says conversation should be "full of grace, seasoned with salt."** What does gracious, interesting speech look like in your daily conversations? What's the opposite of that?
5. **Paul's final words are "Remember my chains. Grace be with you."** Why do you think he wanted them to remember that he was in prison? What does it say about him that his very last word was "grace"?

Paul's letter to the Colossians is complete. He has shown them who Jesus really is, dismantled the false teaching that threatened to pull them away, and painted a picture of the new life that belongs to everyone who is in Christ. But Tychicus carried *two* scrolls to Colossae. The other scroll was a short, personal note tucked alongside the big one. It was addressed to a man named Philemon, and it was about to ask him to do one of the hardest things any person can do.

Turn the page.

7

WELCOME HIM AS YOU WOULD WELCOME ME

Have you seen the movie *Paddington*? A small bear from Peru arrives in London with nothing but a battered suitcase, a floppy hat, and a label around his neck that reads "Please look after this bear. Thank you." He is a stranger in every possible way. He doesn't know how the city works. He doesn't understand British customs. He makes enormous messes wherever he goes. And he has no family, no home, and no one to vouch for him.

The Brown family finds him sitting alone in Paddington Station, and Mrs. Brown decides to take him home. Not because it makes sense. Not because it's convenient. Certainly not because Mr. Brown thinks it's a good idea. Mr. Brown, in fact, spends much of the movie trying to get rid of Paddington. The bear is clumsy. He floods the bathroom. He causes chaos in the kitchen. He attracts the attention of a terrifying taxidermist. Everything about taking this bear into their home is risky, messy, and disruptive.

But Mrs. Brown sees something Mr. Brown doesn't. She sees a person (well, a bear) who needs to be welcomed. And by the end of the film, Mr. Brown sees it too. Paddington doesn't just find a place to sleep. He becomes family. The Browns don't just tolerate him. They claim him. The stranger becomes a son, and the house that reluctantly opened its door is permanently changed for the better.

Paul's letter to Philemon is one of the shortest books in the Bible. It's only twenty-five verses long. You could read it in five minutes. But packed into those twenty-five verses is one of the most powerful real-life examples of the gospel at work that you'll find anywhere in the Bible.

Paul is writing to a man named Philemon, asking him to do something extraordinarily difficult: welcome back a runaway slave named Onesimus, not as a piece of property, but as a brother. And the way Paul makes this request is so carefully crafted, so full of love and wisdom and gentle pressure, that it reads like a masterclass in what it means to live out the gospel in the messiest parts of real life.

THE BACKSTORY

To understand this letter, you need to know the story behind it. Philemon was a Christian who lived in Colossae. He was wealthy enough to own slaves and to host a church in his home. Paul had led him to faith in Christ, probably during one of Paul's stays in Ephesus. The two men knew and loved each other.

Onesimus was one of Philemon's slaves. At some point, Onesimus ran away. He may have stolen money on his way out. In the ancient Roman world, running away was one of the most dangerous things a slave could do. The penalties were severe. If caught, a runaway slave could be beaten, branded, or even killed. Onesimus was taking his life in his hands.

Somehow, whether by accident or by God's quiet direction, Onesimus ended up meeting Paul in prison. And in that prison, Onesimus became a Christian. Paul led him to obey the gospel just as he had led Philemon years earlier. The runaway slave and the imprisoned apostle became as close as a father and son.

Now Paul faced a dilemma. He loved Onesimus and wanted to keep him around as a helper. But he knew that Onesimus needed to go back to Philemon. The broken relationship had to be healed. The wrong had to be addressed. The gospel that Paul preached—the gospel of reconciliation, forgiveness, and new identity in Christ—had to be tested in the real world.

So Paul wrote this letter and sent Onesimus home with it.

GRACE BEFORE THE HARD PART

"Paul, a prisoner of Christ Jesus, and Timothy our brother, To Philemon our dear friend and fellow worker, also to Apphia our sister and Archippus our fellow soldier, and to the church that meets in your home: Grace and peace to you from God our Father and the Lord Jesus Christ."

Notice how Paul introduces himself. He doesn't call himself an apostle, which is his usual title and would carry maximum authority. Instead, he calls himself "a prisoner of Christ Jesus." It's a gentle reminder: I'm writing this from a prison cell. I'm suffering for the same gospel you believe in. This letter carries the weight of someone who has given up everything for Christ.

The letter is addressed to Philemon, but also to Apphia (probably Philemon's wife), Archippus (a fellow Christian, possibly their son or a ministry partner), and "the church that meets in your home." This is important. Paul is writing a personal letter, but he's making sure the whole community hears it. What he's about to ask Philemon to do isn't a private matter. It will affect everyone in the church.

"I always thank my God as I remember you in my prayers, because I hear about your love for all his holy people and your faith in the Lord Jesus. I pray that your partnership in the faith may be effective in deepening your understanding of every good thing we share for the sake of Christ. Your love has given me great joy and encouragement, because you, brother, have refreshed the hearts of the Lord's people."

Before Paul asks for anything, he builds Philemon up. He thanks God for Philemon's love and faith. He highlights Philemon's reputation as someone who "refreshes the hearts" of other believers. This isn't flattery. It's strategy rooted in genuine affection. Paul is reminding Philemon of who he already is: a generous, loving, faithful Christian. He's setting the stage so that what he asks next will feel like a natural extension of what Philemon already does.

THE APPEAL

"Therefore, although in Christ I could be bold and order you to do what you ought to do, yet I prefer to appeal to you on the basis of love."

This is one of the most skillful sentences Paul ever wrote. He tells Philemon he has the authority to give a direct order. He could pull rank. He could command obedience. But he doesn't. Instead, he chooses to appeal on the basis of love. He sets aside his rights in order to make room for Philemon's heart to respond freely.

"It is as none other than Paul, an old man and now also a prisoner of Christ Jesus, that I appeal to you for my son Onesimus, who became my son while I was in chains."

Now the name drops. Onesimus. The runaway slave. The thief (maybe). The source of Philemon's anger and betrayal. Paul doesn't introduce the name right away. He waits until he's established the relational foundation: I'm your friend. I'm in prison. I'm appealing from love. And then: I'm appealing for my son.

"My son." Paul calls Onesimus his child. He became a Christian under Paul's teaching in prison. He's not just a runaway anymore. He's been born again. He's family now.

"Formerly he was useless to you, but now he has become useful both to you and to me." Paul makes a pun here. The name "Onesimus" means "useful." Paul says, in effect, "Your slave 'Useful' used to be useless. Now he's finally living up to his name." It's a moment of gentle humor in an otherwise tense letter. But underneath the wordplay, there's a serious point. Onesimus has been transformed. He's not the same person who ran away.

THE EXCHANGE

"I am sending him, who is my very heart, back to you. I would have liked to keep him with me so that he could take your place in helping me while I am in chains for the gospel. But I did not want to do anything without your consent, so that any favor you do would not seem forced but would be voluntary."

Paul admits he would have loved to keep Onesimus. The young man had become precious to him. But Paul won't go behind Philemon's back. He sends Onesimus home because the relationship between master and slave has to be healed face to face. A reconciliation that only happens at a distance isn't real reconciliation.

Then Paul offers a breathtaking suggestion about why all of this happened in the first place. "Perhaps the reason he was separated from you for a little while was that you might have him back forever, no longer as a slave, but better than a slave, as a dear brother."

Did you catch that? Paul suggests that God may have been working through the whole painful mess. The running away. The separation. The fear and anger. All of it may have been part of God's plan to bring Onesimus to faith and to give Philemon something better than a slave: a brother.

"He is very dear to me but even dearer to you, both as a fellow man and as a brother in the Lord." This is the new reality. Onesimus is no longer just a piece of property. He is a person and a brother. Whatever legal status he holds in the Roman system, his identity in Christ supersedes it. Philemon must now look at the man who wronged him and see a fellow child of God.

PAUL PLAYS CHRIST

"So if you consider me a partner, welcome him as you would welcome me. If he has done you any wrong or owes you anything, charge it to me."

Here is the heart of the letter. Paul does something remarkable. He puts himself in the middle of the broken relationship and absorbs the cost from both sides.

To Philemon he says: treat Onesimus the way you would treat me. If Philemon would welcome Paul with open arms, then he must do the same for Onesimus. They are bound together now, all three of them, in the fellowship of Christ.

And if there's a debt, if Onesimus stole money or damaged property, Paul says: put it on my account. I'll pay it. This is extraordinary. Paul is taking the guilty party's debts onto himself so that the offended party can let go of the grievance.

Does that sound familiar? It should. It's the gospel. Jesus took our debts, our sins, and our failures onto himself so that God could welcome us as beloved children. Paul is doing for Onesimus and Philemon exactly what Christ did for the whole world. He's playing the role of reconciler, standing between two estranged people and absorbing the cost of peace.

"I, Paul, am writing this with my own hand. I will pay it back, not to mention that you owe me your very self."

Paul picks up the pen himself to write this promise. Then, with a twinkle in his eye, he reminds Philemon of a rather significant debt: you owe me your very self. Philemon became a Christian through Paul's ministry. He owes Paul everything. So if Paul is now willing to cover Onesimus' debts, the least Philemon can do is forgive.

"I do wish, brother, that I may have some benefit from you in the Lord; refresh my heart in Christ. Confident of your obedience, I write to you, knowing that you will do even more than I ask."

That last phrase is tantalizing. "Even more than I ask." Paul has asked Philemon to welcome Onesimus as a brother. What would "even more" look like? Many scholars believe Paul is gently hinting that Philemon should set Onesimus free. He doesn't command it. He doesn't even say it directly. But the seed is planted.

ONE MORE THING

"And one thing more: Prepare a guest room for me, because I hope to be restored to you in answer to your prayers."

A final, brilliant touch. Paul is coming to visit. He'll see for himself how Philemon has responded. It's not a threat. It's the promise of a friend who wants to see this reconciliation in person. Paul has invested everything in this situation, and he wants to be there to celebrate when it all comes together.

The letter closes with greetings from the same people mentioned at the end of Colossians: Epaphras, Mark, Aristarchus, Demas, and Luke. And then the final word: "The grace of the Lord Jesus Christ be with your spirit."

Grace. It started with grace. It ends with grace. And everything in between has been an appeal for grace to do its work in the messiest, most painful corner of human life: the place where someone who has wronged you stands in front of you and needs to be forgiven.

WHAT THIS MEANS FOR US

First, the gospel demands reconciliation. It's not enough to believe the right things about Jesus. The gospel has to work itself out in your actual relationships. If there is someone you need to forgive, or someone you need to ask forgiveness from, the message of Philemon says: do it. Not because it's easy, but because Christ has already done it for you.

Second, identity in Christ changes everything. Onesimus was a runaway slave. But in Christ, he became a brother. When you look at other believers, you're not supposed to see their past failures, their social status, or the ways they've wronged you. You're supposed to see someone who belongs to Jesus. That doesn't erase what happened, but it completely reframes how you respond to it.

Third, forgiveness is costly. Paul didn't pretend that Philemon had no reason to be upset. He acknowledged the debt. But then he offered to pay it himself. Real forgiveness always costs somebody something. When you forgive someone, you absorb the loss instead of passing it back. That's painful, but it's what Jesus did for you.

Fourth, God works through the mess. Paul suggested that God may have used Onesimus' running away to bring about something better than what existed before. That doesn't mean God causes people to sin. But it does mean that God is able to take the worst chapters of our stories and weave them into something beautiful. When life seems broken beyond repair, remember: God is still writing.

TALKING POINTS

1. **Paul could have ordered Philemon to forgive Onesimus, but instead he appealed on the basis of love.** Why do you think he chose that approach? What's the difference between doing the right thing because you're told to and doing it because you want to?

2. **Paul told Philemon to welcome Onesimus "no longer as a slave, but as a dear brother."** How does knowing someone

is a fellow Christian change the way you should treat them, especially if they've wronged you?

3. **Paul offered to pay whatever Onesimus owed Philemon.** How does this mirror what Jesus did for us on the cross? Can you think of a time when someone "paid a debt" for you, either literally or figuratively?

4. **Paul hinted that Philemon should do "even more" than what was asked.** What do you think that "more" was? What does it look like to go beyond the minimum when it comes to forgiveness and generosity?

5. **The letter to Philemon is only twenty-five verses long, but it's one of the most personal and practical letters in the Bible.** What's one thing from this letter that you could put into practice in your own relationships this week?

Paul wrote to the Colossians to remind them that Jesus is supreme over everything, that they are complete in him, and that the new life he gives transforms every part of who they are. He wrote to Philemon to show what that new life looks like when it walks through the front door of an actual house and sits down at an actual table across from someone who has actually wronged you.

Together, these two letters paint a picture of a faith that is both cosmic and personal, a faith that holds galaxies together and also heals broken friendships. A faith that defeats the powers of darkness and also forgives a runaway slave. A faith big enough for the throne room of heaven and small enough for Philemon's guest room.

The same Christ who created all things and reconciled all

things is the Christ who lives in you. That's the mystery Paul couldn't stop talking about. That's the hope of glory. And that's the truth that will carry you through every chapter of your own story, if you let it.

The book is finished. Your story is just beginning.

www.ingramcontent.com/pod-product-compliance
Ingram Content Group UK Ltd.
Pitfield, Milton Keynes, MK11 3LW, UK
UKHW020420250726
13967UKWH00007B/2743

9 781971 767314